KEVIN L. LONG

PUT YOUR MASK ON FIRST!

30-Day Devotionals, Meditations, and Affirmations for Evolving Souls

Foreword by Dr. Jamal Harrison-Bryant

The BluPen!
INK. CREATE. LOVE.℠

DEDICATION

*This devotional is dedicated to people committed
to choosing themselves while loving others and
evolving into someone beautiful.*

Hey Fam!
From this day forward,
make sure to Put Your Mask
On First!!!

Much Love and Peace and Many
Blessings

ACKNOWLEDGMENTS

I am convinced that every labor of love is an effort to pay forward the love that the laborer has received from others. Thus, numerous remarkable souls have loved me through this devotional's completion.

First, to the source of all life who loved me enough to become a man like me so I could recapture my true divine creative essence. Heavenly Father, I thank you for eternal life and love in the person of Yeshua the Christ.

Second, to my muse, my purpose partner, my Dark Godiva Chocolate, my wife by day and girlfriend by night, Tarshá Nicole Long, words cannot express how significant your contribution to this project was. Much of the content in this work is inspired by our conversations, shared conflicts, and commitment to hold each other accountable to maximizing our God-given potential and manifesting our God-ordained destiny. I love doing life with you!

To my biological three: my Yakko, my Dot, and my Wacko (Nicholos, Chanel, and Donovan Long). Your love, support, and encouragement to practice self-care in the rough seasons helped me to stay determined to solidify our family legacy. I LOVE Y'ALL!! And to my bonus three: my Ed, Edd, and Eddy (Aaron, Nolan, and Princeton Hamilton), when I married your mom, I found the fountain of youth. Thanks for the sixty thrills a minute EVERY DAY, lol. Love you guys!

To my siblings, nieces, nephews, and cousin-siblings, thank you for your never-ending love, push, and support.

To my TCI family, the past 26 years as your leader have taught me to Put My Mask on First, equipping me to help you put yours on. Thank you for supporting me while I journey through life.

To my sister Chelaé Cummings and The BluPen staff, your commitment to seeing this project through has been a masterclass in excellence and execution. Thank you!

To my friends and colleagues, brothers from another mother, and sisters from another mister, thank you for holding me accountable and administering help to me first when I needed you most.

Lastly, to my social media community who asked when my daily meanderings would become daily meditations, here it is! I hope that you are inspired and blessed.

Much love, peace, and many blessings!

Kevin L. Long

FOREWORD

In this post-pandemic reality, absolutely nothing is normal. We have no track record of God taking his people back to where they used to be. Bishop Long has charted out a GPS in this devotional about the turns we need to make to get closer to God and further from ourselves. The vaccine to hysteria is consistency, and this volume, if followed, will alleviate every strand of anxiety. The booster shot that elevates us past complacency and depression is a lodge in our devotional life. For all of his credentials, research, and training, Dr. Fauci never issued a prescription that would rival what's plastered on these pages. At the height of the pandemic, hospitals were filled to capacity with those who lost the ability to breathe, making intubation their only option. Not too many days into this journey charted by the journal did I begin to exhale with the sigh of release that better days were ahead and God had not forgotten. I charge you to guard this book with your life and treasure it. If the world knew its content, it would be airdropped into every nation as emergency aid. God's favor and grace are now placed in your hand; don't discard it, as the life it saves may very well be your own!

Amazed by His Grace,

Dr. Jamal Harrison Bryant
New Birth Cathedral, Stonecrest, GA

Table of

CONTENTS

MONITOR

ABOUT THE AUTHOR

INTRODUCTION

Hey Fam! Life can be troublesome and frustrating as we navigate these uncharted waters in search of balance post-global pandemic. But with hope, it provides us an opportunity to be innovative when it comes to practicing **SELF-CARE**.

As the world continues and evolves, mandatory mask-wearing is still in effect in some countries. Interestingly, signs guise as public health concerns had discriminatory meanings in reaction to Counterculture Movements such as the 1964 Civil Rights Movement. Signs that read No Shirt, No Shoes, No Service were to keep African-Americans out of restaurants after racial discrimination in the United States became illegal. Those signs have slowly disappeared, but like signs resurfaced during the 2020 global pandemic, warning of imminent public safety concerns reading **NO MASK, NO ENTRY**, and in this case, applied to everyone. These signs operated as reminders when entering stores, hospitals, and etc., to protect yourself and others; wearing a mask has become a choice and necessary precaution.

Living under imposed circumstances where you had to cover your face to live an everyday life is telling to the words of Paul Lawrence Dunbar's poem, "We Wear the Mask." Dunbar compares the pain of oppression to wearing a mask to hide human suffering disguised as a happy face for the world.

For one reason or another, we all wear masks, whether visible or invisible, wanted or unwanted. Masked is a season we've all experienced, and it was deemed necessary for our survival and the survival of others.

If you've ever been on an airplane, you know that every flight begins with safety protocols, and the flight attendant announces what to do in the event cabin pressure drops. "In case of emergency, put your oxygen mask on first before helping others." I believe that following these simple instructions are vital to your survival and to the survival of those who are journeying with you.

This airline metaphor is excellent for those who spend time caring for others while knowingly and unknowingly neglecting themselves. Simply put, if YOU run out of oxygen, you cannot help anyone else with theirs; therefore, taking the time to replenish yourself is critical.

This devotional is designed to help you meditate and affirm your life by providing actionable steps to protect yourself from harm and self-destruction. It is divided into three self-preservation domains: **PERSPECTIVE**, **NURTURE**, and **MONITOR**.

First, "PERSPECTIVE" teaches you how to reframe opposition to see possibilities in place of problems.

Second, "NURTURE" empowers you to develop, manage, and take care of your talents, gifts, and skills.

Lastly, "MONITOR" serves as the self-check system to verify that your progress is on track.

It is important to be forgiving and kind to yourself! Commit yourself, and plan to read, think, and speak the contents of this devotional daily. Write down any thoughts that come to mind while you meditate.

When you awake, before your feet hit the floor or hands reach for your phone, grab this book and **"Put Your Mask on First!"**

PERSPECTIVE

What looks to be
falling apart is actually

FALLING
INTO PLACE

"

Hey Fam! Sometimes it feels like everything around us is
falling apart and it is hard to see the silver lining.

 John 2:19

Being optimistic when it appears that your world
is crumbling can be difficult. Yet everything that
contributes to the dismantling of your life is necessary.
The exciting thing about life is that though at times it appears
to have an illogical or contradictory undertone, everything
always has a way of working itself out. The process of getting
rid of the old to make room for the new or experiencing loss in

order to win feels devastating in moments you have not prepared for. However, hold on to your spirit of expectation! The process of divine improvement includes deconstruction and reconstruction. In John 2:19, Jesus says, "Destroy this temple and I will raise it again in three days."

God has the uncanny ability to work through the rubble of our lives to construct something far greater than we could imagine. If you feel like you are in the thick of it, or that a whirlwind is ravaging your life, remember to trust the process. The pieces of your life are coming together to build a better you. When things fall apart choose not to wallow, instead, be thankful for what is being built. Life is about learning important lessons.

Remember that God will help you pick up the pieces. You can choose to put them back together or build something new, but TRUST THE PROCESS! Trusting the process while going through it is one of the hardest things to do. But understanding the function and timing of God's plan in your life gives you an edge knowing that things are falling into place.

AFFIRMATION

*Life is better than ever because
everything is falling into place.*

_____

_____

Settling is a form of

SELF-
HATRED

"

Hey Fam! Low self-esteem will have you
reaching for low hanging fruit.

 Luke 15:11-17

Comfortability is the low-hanging fruit that causes you not to reach the height of your potential or the power of your purpose. Please don't settle for a life in a low place; rather, confront it to get to higher ground.

Confronting low self-esteem means you have to be honest with yourself, especially in moments when you are feeling uncomfortable and less confident. During those low moments it is important that you do not lose sight of reality. Whether you are dealing with the bombardment of outward criticism, or your inner thoughts echoing that you are not good enough, it's important to silence the negative noise in order to see yourself positively. God didn't create you to settle for less than a fruitful life. You were created to do phenomenal things! Settling is counterintuitive to your greatness.

When low self-esteem or depression comes knocking, don't answer. Instead, meditate on God's love for you and that He calls you blessed. It is this towering truth that dispels the lies of low self-esteem. God filters through the circumstances of our lives to remind us of His presence and partnership. You do not have to be held hostage in mental anguish, captivated by lies.

Starting today, make a mental shift from low self-esteem by acknowledging that you are an heir of God. Your inheritance is greater than what you may have squandered in your past seasons of devaluing yourself. Nothing can separate you from the love of the Father; He's interwoven into your life. Begin speaking life into yourself. Say what your Heavenly Father says about you! You are unique and worthy. He's crazy about you!

AFFIRMATION

I will not settle for less, but I will reach for more!

_____

_____

*Some of your greatest
victories were in your*

PRIVATE
BATTLES

"

Hey Fam! Private battles are often the things
that everyone is not privy to, but the things that
prepare us for public victories.

 1 Samuel 17:32-37

Tackling the private battles of your life can include
getting out of bed every morning, fulfilling callings,
dealing with family problems, health issues, financial
challenges, and much more. Celebrating yourself for showing
up publicly after surviving what should have killed you
privately is commendable.

We all have battles, some bigger than others. You may privately deal with loneliness, depression, unmet expectations, abuse, hurt, or physical challenges. Nevertheless, we handle them the best we can.

Moreover, private battles create the most significant opportunities for us to hone the skills necessary to face impending battles.

Private battles are the breeding ground for public wins, and while they are overwhelming, they teach us to take things step-by-step, and, day-by-day, how to show up for life as a winner.

Keep showing up!!! You are being forged by fire!!!

AFFIRMATION

*I will face private battles fiercely
knowing I always win.*

_____

_____

_____

_____

*They either
sharpen your edge or*

DULL YOUR SHINE

❝

Hey Fam! Who surrounds you?
Are you in good company?

Proverbs 27:17 & Proverbs 30:15

As you go through life, being mindful of the company you keep is crucial. Who you choose to spend our time with is telling. If you think of yourself as a metal blade and everyone else is a stone, you are either sharpened, polished, or dulled by those with whom you interact. The people in your life either drive you to excellence or drain you of energy. Choose wisely!

You need to be aware of the people around you. They may have been great before, but today they might not be going in the same direction. Being intentional about the relationships in your life is necessary to maintain peace.

The scriptural maxim presents an undeniable truth; iron sharpens iron. Iron is a specific metal. Like metals sharpen like metals. Like people sharpen like people. The dissonance comes when the friction of the sharpening is not conducive to us. You need people like you to sharpen you. Are you surrounding yourself with people of iron or people of paper?

Do you know the paper people in your life?

Knives become dull through regular use, and the blade is no longer as sharp. As you cut with them, they wear down. To sharpen knives, honing steel must be used. Using the wrong material can dull your blade. There is no in-between. For good measure, ask yourself, do the people around you sharpen or dull you?

AFFIRMATION

❖ ❖ ❖

Stay sharp!

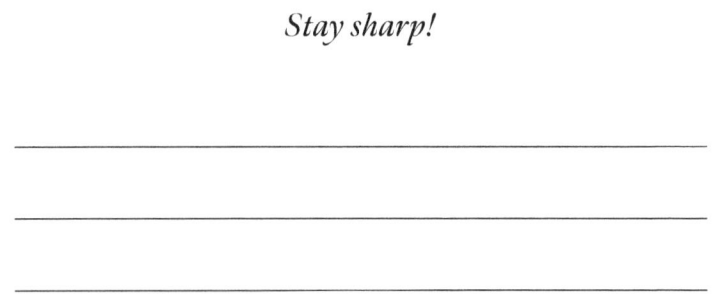

*The more you pray about
it the less you should*

STRESS
ABOUT IT

❝

Hey Fam! You may have heard this before, so here's your
gentle reminder. If you are going to pray don't worry, and
if you are going to worry don't pray!

📖 Philippians 4:6

Fear, worry, and anxiety are harmful forces that distract people from living freely. These emotions often leave people overwhelmed mentally and even emotionally paralyzed. To avoid extended stays in these dark and dismal dungeons of painful emotions, we should all commit to praying without ceasing. Prayer is simply communicating with God, and it positions you to receive all you need from Him.

Stress and worry are the antithesis of prayer and release. There is no need to worry when you pray.

Prayer provides the confidence that God has everything in control and helps combat the stress of feeling like you are navigating life alone. When you pray, you exchange your anxiety for the power of God to be at work in your life. When you pray, you show the Most High that you have confidence that He hears you. As you make it a consistent practice to connect with Him, it will encourage you to pray immediately when fear, anxiety, stress, or worry tries to weigh you down.

If you feel powerless, pray. If you feel stressed, pray. If you feel anxious, pray. If you feel worried, pray. Pray for the best, and watch serenity, peace, and clear direction emerge as a result.

AFFIRMATION

I will pray with confidence because I know that when I pray, the Most High hears me.

_____

_____

_____

_____

Sometimes you win by

REFUSING TO FIGHT

“

Hey Fam! It has been said, “You do not have to attend every argument that you're invited to.”

✝ 2 Chronicles 20:14-17

Being selective about what and who you entertain in your sensitive, birthing, or growing season is ok. Mature people recognize when things are going awry. Recognizing the tell-tale signs at the onset of dangerous and potentially detrimental energy trying to invade your space is essential, and paying attention to details that you discern spiritually is using wisdom.

Sometimes the Most High shows you the enemy's activity so that you can sit in a front-row seat just to watch Him fight your battles. God already knows the outcome; His plan promises you prosperity, good health, and a future. That being the case, if you trust in Him and the promises that He has made to you, you can rest knowing that you will always win your battles in the end. Essentially, it is a sweatless victory!

When life presents a battle, you can respond with confidence, stillness, and silence that you don't have to fight. Despite popular belief, your refusal or conscious decision to not fight is not a sign of weakness; instead, it is a sign that you have "insider" information.

Hold your peace and let the Lord fight your battles, for the battle belongs to the Lord. No weapon formed against you shall prosper!

AFFIRMATION

❖ ❖ ❖

I always win!

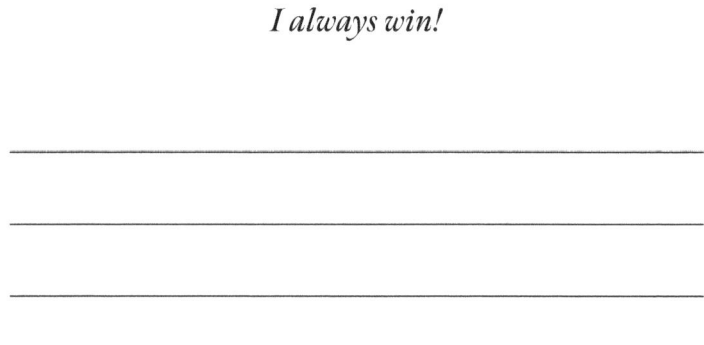

Champions

IGNORE THE CHATTER

Hey Fam! Ignore the critics.

 Philippians 3:2-14 & Romans 14:4

Ignoring the chatter is easier said than done, especially when the talk gets the best of you and lives rent-free in your head. Learning to master the art of silencing negative voices can take some time, but the more you practice silencing distractions, the better your life will be. Never allow the criticism of those clamoring to distract you from your purpose to claim the real estate of your mind.

Those with the most to say through negative criticisms, judgments, and opinions are most often miserable and threatened by your manifesting a purpose beyond their scope. With that in mind, remember that you are chosen to fulfill a need, answer a problem, and do great work in the world.

Be mindful of what you let into your ears, and listen to a positive frequency that uplifts and speaks to the champion in you. Deafen your ears to the static of the frequencies lower than the expectations set for yourself. You are vibrating higher for a reason.

AFFIRMATION

As a champion, I will only listen to voices vibrating on a higher frequency of success.

You're only a failure if you fail to

LEARN FROM YOUR FAILURES

"

Hey Fam! Failure is an opportunity to learn.

✚ Proverbs 24:15-16

L earning occurs when the consequence(s) of behavior create(s) new and better actions from you. The key to growth is to have a healthy perspective concerning the intrinsic value of failure.

Accepting failure with a loathing frame of mind will cause you to miss it as an opportunity to fail, fall or feel your way forward.

Seeing failure as an indicator of growth will allow you to recognize that failure is not final. Likewise, by seeing failure through the lens of change as a buoyant aid moving you towards success, you will quickly learn the power of resilience. Knowing that you are not limited to your last moment of failure will allow you to use failure as a catalyst toward self-mastery.

In some instances, failing to learn from your mistakes may be an issue of cognitive dissonance. Albert Einstein was definitely on to something when he said that doing the same thing repeatedly (over and over), expecting different results, is insanity.

AFFIRMATION

❖ ❖ ❖

Failure is not a fact. I will recognize the
opportunity in failure to grow towards success.

Whatever stretches you,

STRENGTHENS YOU

Hey Fam! Faith is tested through trials.

📖 James 1:2-4

Trials can almost stretch us to the point of breaking down. When you are near your breaking point, the stretching of life's trials should not cause you to falter under the weight of a problem—instead, remain.

The Greek word hupomone comes from 'hupo' (under) and 'meno' (to stay, abide, remain); at its root, it means to remain under. Imagine you're under a heavy load; instead of running away, you stay under it. The strength and conditioning training ground for a breakthrough is to remain calm, still, or in the situation with things causing you pressure, pain or hardship.

To gain strength, you will be stretched past your limits and won't break. Do not avoid difficulty in life. Allow its temporary discomfort to produce in you the strength needed to abide through the trial to pass the test.

AFFIRMATION

I will endure and remain no matter what comes my way.

_____

_____

_____

_____

NURTURE

Opposition announces the

ARRIVAL OF OPPORTUNITY

"

Hey Fam! Opportunity is knocking,
and it has brought a guest.

 1 Corinthians 16:9

Everything is going fine in your life when an uninvited guest knocks on the door. Expecting no one, you peep out the window to see who it is, but they look obscure. You crack the door, discovering that opposition has arrived, taken by surprise, you shut the door quickly. DJ cue Little Richard's "Keep a Knockin." I know you are side-eyeing life right now like, who invited them? When opposition knocks, opportunity answers.

How you choose to see things makes all of the difference. The word opposition, in most cases, is perceived as problematic, but you can choose to respond to opposition without panic or disdain. Right now, there are countless challenges facing the world—collectively and individually. You can focus on the elements of your problems—the things you can't do, the limitations, the losses, the lack of something. Or, you can acknowledge the opposition, hear the opportunity in the announcement, and focus on the hidden possibilities for personal growth, development, and holistic prosperity. A life of abundance awaits you on the other side of what stands between you and your next phase of manifested destiny. When facing any opposition, always ask yourself, IS THERE SOMETHING FOR ME TO LEARN IN THIS SITUATION?

By the way, don't be rude; this is your opportunity to answer!

AFFIRMATION

I will not be overwhelmed by opposition. Instead I will be present, knowing that opposition is the breeding ground for opportunity!

_____

_____

_____

Refuse to come down to the level of the people who are trying to

PULL YOU DOWN

Hey Fam! You give your power away when you pay attention to adversaries, detractors, and naysayers.

Nehemiah 6:1-3

Getting lost in the negative commentary of critics can be a long trip down the rabbit hole. Nowadays, more than ever, we are more susceptible to hearing or reading what others say about us. Not giving in to the knee-jerk reaction to respond in kind to someone with the same energy is a skill that many haven't mastered. Tune them out! The fact that you're the object of their attention means that your life is far more interesting and exciting to them than the life that they are living. You are too busy and too productive to condescend to those with low-level thinking.

Learn to maintain your position; while using their harsh criticism as a tool to propel you forward personally and professionally. Use the force of negativity intended to pull you down as a slingshot to shoot you to an elevated, more positive version of yourself; people won't see it coming. Use foul feedback as fuel. Keep rising!

AFFIRMATION

*I refuse to come down! I refuse to stoop to their level.
I will rise above the negative commentary.*

_____

_____

_____

_____

Faith is the ability to
focus in the midst of

FIERY
TRIALS

❝

Hey Fam! When everything around you appears
to be chaotic, your confidence in the Divine should
serve as an anchor within you.

 James 1:2-4

Although it may not feel like it now, you are chosen. Out of all the people in the world, God created you to do the great things He has purposed ONLY YOU to do. Thus far, you have survived 100% of everything the enemy designed to destroy you. You should be proud of yourself. You are an overcomer!

God chose you to make His name great.

When you encounter fiery trials of any magnitude, don't falter or wane. Instead, be thankful that God chose you to stand fearlessly in the face of adversity. Moreover, be joyful, knowing that trials create something far more powerful in you than what is apparent right now.

AFFIRMATION

I have faith to face fiery trials ferociously!

_____

_____

_____

_____

You should be your most

RELIABLE ENCOURAGER

❝

Hey Fam! If you give others the ultimate
power to validate your importance, value, and
worth you will be sadly disappointed.

📖 1 Samuel 30:6

It is great to receive accolades from others. We all enjoy
the recognition that boosts our esteem, but what happens
when those who should applaud you want to destroy you?

One of the most devastating realities in life is recognizing that
those who once supported you have turned their backs on you.
One moment they cheer you on, and the next, they verbally

chop you down. That's a harsh yet unavoidable truth.

What do you do?

When you get hurt, to protect yourself from the pain that comes with the disappointment of betrayal, there is a natural inclination to resign and retreat. I admonish you to fight the easy preference to withdraw from the world and encourage yourself out of the situation. Encourage yourself by knowing who you are and whose you are.

Your self-worth should never be predicated on those who do or do not support you.

AFFIRMATION

I will encourage myself, knowing that
I am important, valuable and capable!

_____

_____

_____

_____

Generational curse breakers

CAN'T BE BROKEN

Hey Fam! Everything intended to
break you will be broken.

John 2:19-22

The power in you is greater than the powers working against you. Some people believe that where you come from, who you come through, and what bloodline you inherit determine your final makeup. In most cases, we would agree that these things determine how we adapt or change throughout our lives.

But in every bloodline, a person is born with the power to break curses and cycles of mental, physical, financial, emotional, and spiritual drought in a family. You have gone through absolute hell, only to discover you are a champion. Created with layers of unknown and raw materials, fortitude, grit, and more. Therefore, you are UNBREAKABLE!!!

The power in you will alleviate generational curses, break through boundaries, and shatter repeated patterns. Live in your authority and ability to break everything sent to destroy generations after you. Tap into the reservoir of the breaker in you because curse breakers can't be broken.

AFFIRMATION

There is a breaker authority that resides within me. I will operate within the authority that the Most High has given me.

_____

_____

_____

_____

The one who is willing to let everything go is the one who will eventually

HAVE IT ALL

"

Hey Fam! The ability to selflessly detach from the outcome of your efforts proves to the Most High that He can trust you with blessings and favor.

 1 Kings 3:16-28 & Ecclesiastes 11:1

Society programs us to hustle, build, create and amass a lot of things to be happy. If we're honest, we often buy into that same system to acquire the necessary things for the life we believe we want and deserve. Sometimes, once we achieve it all, we are still not happy, but letting it go is like starting over.

Recognizing that your value is not in material earnings happens when your temporal realm releases and collides with the supernatural. Your courage to release everything will position you to open your storehouse to receive the cornucopia of blessings always meant for you.

Essentially, the Most High works to give us above all that we can ask or think. Be open to receiving the divine manifestation of your desires. What's yours is yours! You won't have to manipulate situations to get it or orchestrate conditions to keep it!

AFFIRMATION

*Today, I release everything so that
I am in a position to have it all!*

*Relationships that
refine you positively*

REDEFINE YOU

"

Hey Fam! The proof of the proper interpersonal connection is when challenges and confrontations in our relationships result in positive change.

✝ Proverbs 27:17 & Luke 5:1-11

The only constant thing in life is change. Change is the byproduct of intentionality. How you approach, interpret, and respond to the occurance of conflict, friction, or disagreement with people in your life determines your growth. After a confrontation, your behavior indicates your willingness to acquiesce to the challenge to repair or release a relationship.

Change and challenge in your relationships should move you to sift through the areas of perception and character that need work in your life. It doesn't always mean to end a relationship but to examine its value more closely. Setting intentions to see yourself through positive and negative interactions with others is a form of self-love and maturity.

There is a saying that people come into your life for a reason, season, or lifetime. Regardless of their role and time, it is essential to remain open to the lesson— anyone who helps you morph into the best version of yourself has helped to redefine you.

AFFIRMATION

I seek to develop relationships that are supportive and intentional.

_____

_____

_____

_____

You have the benefit of

INVISIBLE ALLIES

❝

Hey Fam! Never underestimate the power of angelic
assistance and divine reinforcement.

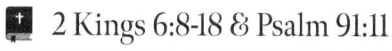

✝ 2 Kings 6:8-18 & Psalm 91:11

D o you believe in angels? Believe it or not, angels
are a vital part of our everyday lives even though
we cannot see them. Angels always carry out the
Most High's plan and purpose and are here to provide divine
enablement. Our deliverance and protection come from the
divine reinforcement they provide us.

As Angels were present to aid those during biblical times, angels are with us. Elisha explained this to his servant when the Syrian army surrounded them. The servant was afraid, but Elisha said, "Do not fear, for those who are with us are more than those who are with them, (2 Kings 6:16 NKJV)." When the servant opened his spiritual eyes, he saw an army of angels and chariots of fire surrounding the entire Syrian army.

Open your spiritual eyes to see angelic assistance assigned to your life when you feel surrounded by all your problems and cannot see your way out.

AFFIRMATION

May my spiritual eyes be open to seeing angelic assistance and divine reinforcement.

_____

_____

_____

_____

Never underestimate the gift of

ANOTHER CHANCE

66

Hey Fam! Waking up to another day is God's way of
allowing you to make self-improvements.

✝ Lamentations 3:21-23 & Isaiah 43:18

C arpe diem (seize the day)! You must eagerly take the
day or the moment as if it is your last opportunity to
succeed.

The good book describes life as a vapor. James 4:14 (The
Passion Translation) says, "Your life is but a warm breath of
air that is visible in the cold only for a moment then vanishes."

This verse teaches us that tomorrow is not promised, and life should not be taken for granted.

The transience of life is such that days on this earth are fleeting. It is essential to recognize life's brevity so you do not squander it. You get another chance to improve each day you receive the gift of life. Live intentionally in the eternal now, and work on your purpose daily. Living in the now will keep you focused on the things that matter for eternity.

AFFIRMATION

I will seize life and maximize living.

_____

_____

_____

_____

Self-improvement is the debt that you owe to the people who accept you for

WHO YOU ARE

Hey Fam! Unconditional love and acceptance should inspire continual personal development.

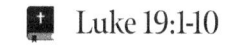

Luke 19:1-10

Becoming a better person is having a positive self-concept. "Good, better, best. Never let it rest. Until your good is better and your better is best." Growing up, I heard this saying to inspire me to develop who I was from the inside out.

Accepting yourself entirely in your flawed and flawless moments lets you practice unconditional inward love directly. In doing so, you can give of yourself to those you have a relationship with and evolve together. Properly aligning your authentic self with the experiences you create with others is a vital ingredient to who you were, are, and will become.

Understanding there is much to be said for expressing appreciation for the unconditional love and acceptance you receive from others, no matter what version you present on any given day. Express your gratitude to them for loving and accepting you without exception by committing to a lifestyle of consistent self-betterment.

AFFIRMATION

I possess a high self-value, and my relationships align with my core values.

_____

_____

_____

_____

Give the understanding that you

WISH TO RECEIVE

"

Hey Fam! Requiring forgiveness more readily than you are willing to give it is an arrogance that inevitably ends in psycho-emotional torment.

 Matthew 18:21-35

Unforgiveness is a hamster wheel of emotional anguish that disrupts your physical and mental energy—embracing the gift of understanding and forgiveness teaches you how to become tolerant and sympathetic towards others. Being misunderstood can be frustrating and annoying, but committing to understanding is a gateway to thoughtfulness. Adopting a mindset of understanding opens your awareness to sense when others are hurting or need support. A decision to forgive allows you to achieve a level of vulnerability necessary to heal deep personal emotional wounds that could hinder your overall spiritual and emotional growth. When you extend understanding and forgiveness to others, it postures you to receive it reciprocally. Give others what you have longed to obtain and remain postured to receive a bountiful harvest.

AFFIRMATION

Today, I commit to understanding others considering how I want to be understood.

_____

_____

_____

_____

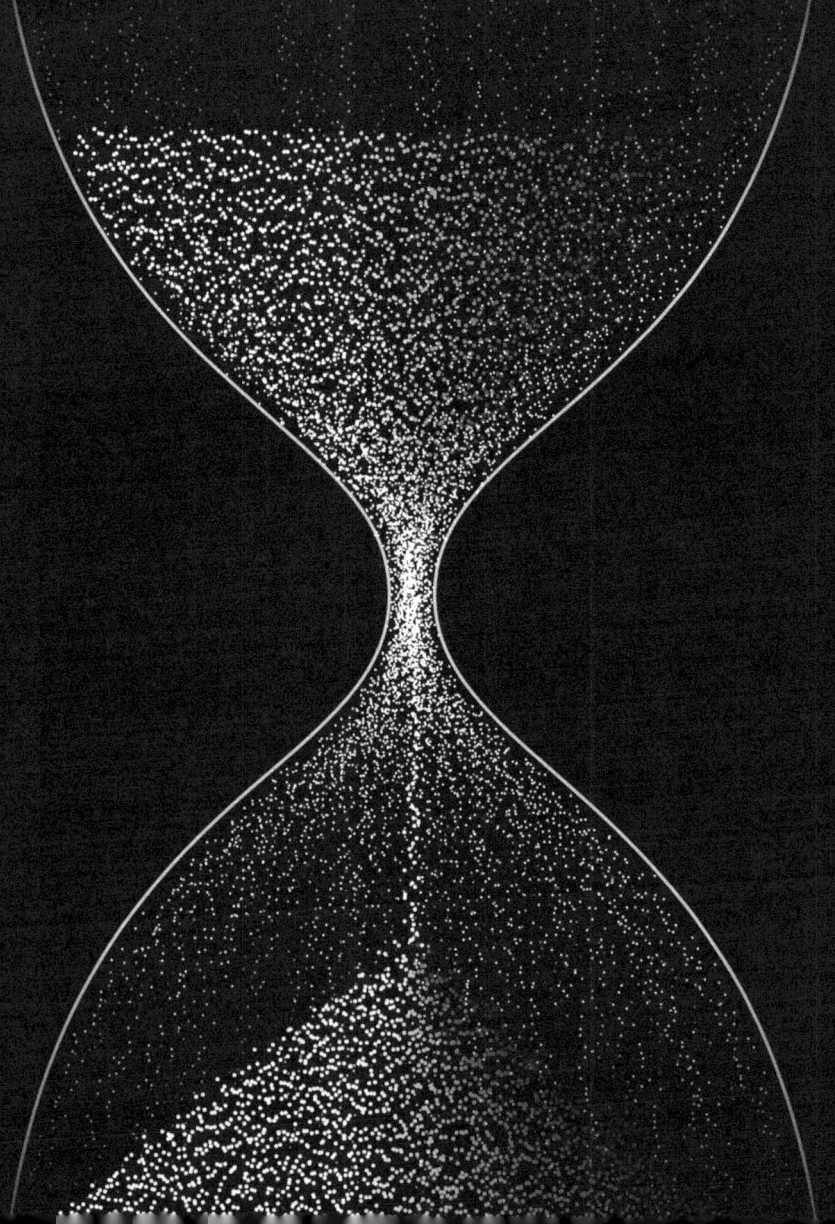

MONITOR

Forward thinkers have
mastered the art of putting

THE PAST
BEHIND THEM

" "

Hey Fam! You can't get ahead looking backwards.

✝ Luke 9:62 & Philippians 3:13-14

Reflection is a way to process the past, but don't get stuck there. Sometimes you have to fast forward through past pain to protect your future. Looking back will cause you to miss what is in front of you. Becoming a forward thinker happens when you master the art of acceptance of your past and present without allowing them to affect your future negatively.

In life, we all go through things that we would have preferred not to experience, but the truth is every step we take, every experience we have, and every moment good or bad, places us in front of a new entry or exit. It is up to you to walk through the new doors in front of you.

There will be times when you have to look back to appreciate how far you've come and how much you've grown. Moving forward requires focusing on what is before you to possess your future — a "prize" that awaits you! And WHAT A PRIZE IT IS!!!

AFFIRMATION

I will keep moving forward. What's ahead of me is greater than what's behind me.

_____

_____

_____

_____

It's okay to admit that

YOU'RE NOT OKAY

❝

Hey Fam! Don't let your greatest weakness be that you're always trying to prove that you're strong.

 Matthew 26:36-38

Real strength lies in the ability to be self-aware. Emotionally intelligent individuals can acknowledge that they are not okay. Despite your pain, you must show up for all your emotional experiences. If you don't accept the reality of every single occasion, they will continue to show up in your life differently. Repeated cycles of the same trauma cause you to dismiss your natural ability to heal correctly subconsciously. Actively processing your emotions allows you to heal and gives you healthy strength and perspective to see yourself and situations creatively. It is not always comfortable to embrace or share that you are in a vulnerable moment. If you have not done so, release the thought that feeling pain means being weak or doing something wrong and forgive yourself. Admitting that you're not okay means shedding the shame of needing help to attract the love and support you need to be revived, survive, and thrive in the life you have ahead of you.

AFFIRMATION

Today, I am released from the shame of not being ok and I am free to feel and heal!

Sometimes your most detrimental liability is

YOUR ACCESSIBILITY

"

Hey Fam! Don't get so consumed with meeting the needs of others that you forget to take care of yourself.

 Mark 6:30-32

Energy vampires and boundary busters are real! Choosing self-care is not selfish. Your emotional, mental, and physical health matters more than you understand. Protecting your peace and safeguarding your environment is required to maintain a healthy mental state. Reducing accessibility to people and situations that take your energy allows you to control your space. We often participate in our demise unintentionally: Your phone rings, and you pick it up immediately. You get an email, text, or social media alert, and you stop what you are doing to respond.

These actions indicate that you may be too accessible and are giving up your time to care for your own needs. You cannot be everything to everyone if you are not first to yourself. Invariably someone will be disappointed, but it's time to stop being so available! Finding the perfect balance of being warm and generous while taking care of yourself and prioritizing your time comes when you understand and abide by your limits.

AFFIRMATION

I only have so much time! I only have so much energy! I only have so much space to use to my maximum ability.

_____

_____

_____

_____

Growth is accepting 100% of the

RESPONSIBILITY FOR YOUR LIFE

❝

Hey Fam! Self-accountability will prevent you from granting authority to or shifting blame onto others as it relates to the outcomes you experience in life.

✝ Luke 23:39-43 & Galatians 6:4-5

M any books have been written on personal growth. If you browse any bookstore's personal development or self-improvement section, you will see hundreds if not thousands of books on the subject. One of the most important decisions you can make is to constantly improve and become a better version of yourself.

Embracing the idea that you are not what you have done but you are who you work at becoming on an hourly, daily, monthly, or yearly account is taking full accountability for your actions. Your journey to becoming a better human is a lifelong experience in which you don't know what your next adventure will yield.

Taking responsibility for your be-haviors, thoughts, words, and actions can be as simple as looking inward to identify negative self-talk and replacing it with positive affirmations. You can level up by learning something new, setting realistic targeted goals, and planning to achieve them with implementable steps. Your life is yours to own, develop and reconstruct 100%.

AFFIRMATION

I will be better today than I was yesterday!

Don't let their labels

LIMIT YOU

66

Hey Fam! You're too multi-dimensional to be defined
by people with a one-dimensional vision.

✝ Mark 6:1-8 & Mark 8:27-29

Labels are not lifelong. We live in a society where
people quickly label you based on misunderstanding
who you are—limiting you to what they believe,
your past, or their perception of your depth. Once labeled,
they leave you there conditionally to hold you back. It
is important to extend grace to yourself as you live out
the layers of your personality and to resist agreeing or

labeling yourself.

You may sometimes feel the urge to succumb to the labels imposed on you, but you have the power to take back the narrative of your life. Labels affixed to your character, personality, or lifestyle by society or people are not always accurate. Do not allow your persona to be limited, defined, or controlled by damaging labels. Labels interwoven and introduced through society happen as early as grade school and exist within our family structures.

Harmful labels do not align with who the Most High created you to be or who He says you are. You can choose not to answer the limitations of labels that don't fit how you see yourself.

In your journey to healing from labels, titles, or words placed on you by your family, teachers, friends, job, ego, and so on, remember it's your responsibility to change your beliefs and exit from living within those labels. You are not a victim of your past or labels. Self-affirm and teach the world how to see and speak about you.

AFFIRMATION

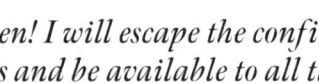

I will stay open! I will escape the confining box of labels and be available to all that the Most High has for me!

_____

_____

_____

Give yourself the gift of
FORGIVENESS

Hey Fam! One of the primary keys to achieving inner peace, spiritual wholeness, and continuing in your God-ordained purpose is to learn the art of forgiving yourself.

1 Samuel 30:1-8

We can be our harshest critics because we hold ourselves to high standards. What happens when you let yourself down? Is there a plan in place for how you forgive or regain respect for yourself? Most often, the answer is no, and we don't even see ourselves as worthy of forgiveness. Sometimes it's easier to forgive others, to avoid facing the fears of our mistakes or shortcomings towards ourselves. Choose to be kind to yourself. Do not continue to beat yourself up subconsciously. If you have made mistakes in the past, it's easy to be overly critical of yourself.

The real meaning of forgiveness is to make a conscious, deliberate decision to release feelings of resentment or vengeance toward a person or group who has harmed you, regardless of whether they deserve your forgiveness. You, too, deserve forgiveness. Practicing self-forgiveness also helps you see yourself as human and worthy to receive forgiveness.

Forgiving yourself requires effort, humility, compassion, and understanding. That list of people to forgive includes YOU TOO!!!

AFFIRMATION

I have chosen to release myself from past mistakes and any future mistakes. I am forgiven and will live my life as a forgiven person.

_____

_____

_____

_____

The only thing that you
have to prove is that you have

NOTHING
TO PROVE

66

Hey Fam! If the only way that you feel good about
yourself is when you have the acceptance and approval
of others, you will always have a miserable life.

 Matthew 11:16-19

W anting to please people is a natural human
behavior. However, without limitations, it could
be detrimental to your productivity and life's
purpose. Some people thrive off of what others think about
them, while others live in anguish and get stuck. The truth is
that there will always be someone in this world who is "better"
than you, "more intelligent" than you, "wealthier" than you.

Comparing the worst version of yourself with your best perception of them is not fair to you. The standards that you set for yourself are all that matter.

Prove means demonstrating the truth or existence of (something) by evidence or argument. You don't have to argue or prove who you are or can be. The sooner you realize that you have nothing to prove, the better your life will be.

Your life will transform for the better when you stop trying to impress, stack up to, or compare yourself to other people and live authentically.

AFFIRMATION

I realize that I have nothing to prove.
I will stop trying to impress others and live
authentically as myself.

*Don't be the person
who dies before you stop*

BREATHING

Hey Fam! When death finally catches you,
it should be out of breath!

Ecclesiastes 8:15

Have you ever noticed that your pace slows when you are about to complete a task? Self-sabotage and worry in all aspects of life, again and again, cause us to fall short when we are on the cusp of greatness.

There was an experienced ultramarathon runner a few feet from the finish line. His legs buckled beneath him as the crowd watched his slow-motion tumble to the ground. He collapsed from physical exhaustion even though he had trained and prepared for the race. While there could have been other medical issues, it's clear that he ran out of energy. However, the story doesn't end with his collapse. Though he crumbled to the ground, he crawled across the finish line.

As you run through the streets, marathons, or obstacle courses of life, remember some races require a jog, others are a sprint. Some are long distances, and some are one hurdle after another. Some-times you might unsuccessfully measure the height of a hurdle, causing you to stumble and fall. In those times, redefine that pit-fall as a pitstop, get yourself to-gether and GET BACK UP!!! Whatever the case, it is essential to remember to pace your breath through each terrain. Life may feel like it will kill you but keep running until it gets tired of chas-ing you through your victories. Even if you don't cross the finish line IMMEDIATELY, you will cross it EVENTUALLY! You are a winner and deserve to live your life to the fullest!

AFFIRMATION

I will maintain the momentum to live life to the fullest.

_____

_____

_____

*In order to make your
life easier, you have to*

MAKE HARD DECISIONS

❝

Hey Fam! Experiencing the manifestation of
destiny is largely dependent upon making difficult
decisions in difficult times.

📖 2 Kings 7:3-8 & 1 Kings 7:16-28

At some point in life, we all encounter a fork in
the road when we come face-to-face with making a drastic or difficult decision. Sometimes it happens more than once if you are evolving and elevating into the best version of yourself. How you handle these moments can impact all areas of your life, including the lives of those around you. At this point,

you must know and discern opportunities that require you to take calculated risks.

Pondering difficult decisions can bring thoughts of tension and confusion. It is grossly immature to make decisions only considering the present moment. Life will continue beyond that one decision or moment based on what you set in motion for yourself and those you are responsible for leading or love. Knowing the difference between a head choice and a heart choice is of the utmost importance. A head choice makes sense on paper, but a heart choice speaks to your soul by meeting a need or longing.

AFFIRMATION

I am graced with the power to make difficult decisions in difficult times.

_____

_____

_____

_____

The key to having
limitless peace is to have

DEFINITE BOUNDARIES!

Hey Fam! If you value serenity and tranquility, you must master the art of controlling the amount of access that you give to your emotional, physical, and spiritual spaces.

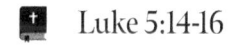

Luke 5:14-16

S etting boundaries is hard work! You may wonder if they are worth the effort if people continue to cross them. The answer is yes! Boundaries are the guidelines that teach others how to treat you. A boundary can be a request for someone to change behavior that you consider disrespectful toward you or a safeguard that you put in place to keep people from "pushing your buttons" or "flipping your switch." The critical thing to remember is that you are in control during both situations and have the explicit right to push people back over the boundary line.

A boundary is defined by your capacity to accept or receive what others bring into your personal space. You must do everything possible to keep your peace of mind and ensure a tranquil environment. "Toxic" is a word or behavior that this generation has popularized as a form of acceptance to keep people in your life who trespass against your boundaries repeatedly. Toxic peo-

ple become harmful over time and eventually decay your ability to control your emotional, physical, and spiritual movements. Many people are learning to live with what others present them at the expense of limiting themselves while erasing boundaries set to protect their space....DON'T LET THAT BE YOU!!!

Relationships work when we are transparent, know our expectations and needs, and hold fast to them. To enjoy beauty and abundance in your relationships, bless yourself and others with the gift of BOUNDARIES!

AFFIRMATION

❖ ❖ ❖

I will establish and maintain healthy
boundaries in my life.

_____

_____

About
THE AUTHOR

Kevin L. Long is a modern-day "Renaissance Man" and third-generation preacher and pastor. He has traveled the world for over 25 years, sharing the Gospel of Jesus Christ through sermons, lectures, workshops, and spiritual mentoring. He is the Senior Pastor of Temple Church International in Charlotte, NC.

He is a social activist and former Site Coordinator for the Southern Christian Leadership Conference (SCLC) National AIDS education program. The program offered education to the Black community on HIV/AIDS transmission and protection. Kevin helped build collaborative relationships with churches and the community to develop attitudes and environments of compassion for those living with HIV/AIDS and their families.

Kevin has been an active voice and advocate for education and Social Justice reform on local, state, and national platforms. Kevin organized community leaders, clergy, businesses, and gang members from North and South Carolina, spearheading Charlotte's first Christian leader, "Kneel in Protest," at the Bank of America Carolina Panthers NFL stadium in 2017. This protest was one of the largest gatherings of over 150 people in support of kneeling during the National Anthem, a movement started by former NFL player Colin Kaepernick against brutality, killing, and aggressive policing toward black and brown communities. Without hesitation, protesters came together from all walks of life neutrally on a unified message.

In 2013, Kevin was the Co-Executive Producer on "The Sisterhood," the first faith-based reality show to air nationally on TLC in the United States and internationally in South Africa. The controversial show focused on the lives of four preacher wives in Atlanta and opened doors for this reality TV genre of shows like Pastors Daughters and the franchise Preachers of LA, Detroit, and Atlanta.

Kevin is a Stellar Award-nominated songwriter, having written "Great Is Your Faithfulness" on "Praise Revisited," recorded by gospel legend Bishop Larry Trotter and The Sweet Holy Spirit Choir of Chicago.

To learn more about Kevin, keep up with his author's journey, or invite him to speak at your event, ministry, or organization, please visit www.kevinllong.com.

www.ingramcontent.com/pod-product-compliance
Lightning Source LLC
Chambersburg PA
CBHW051643120626
46551CB00015B/2195